# THE CHINESE INVENT
# The Compass

Kevin Fitch

CRAZY COOL CHINA



ROSEN PUBLISHING
NEW YORK

SinolinguA
华语教学出版社
BEIJING

Jointly published in 2021 by Sinolingua Co., Ltd., Beijing, China, and
The Rosen Publishing Group, Inc., New York, New York, United States



First Edition

Editor: John Kemmerer
Designer: Rachel Rising

Photo credits: Cover, pp. 4, 8, 12, 16, 20, 24, 28, 32, 36, 40 ViewStock/Getty Images; p. 5 Zhang Peng/LightRocket/Getty Images; p. 6 Prostock-studio/Shutterstock.com; p. 9 British Library; p. 10 Universal History Archive/Universal Images Group/Getty Images; p. 13 Science & Society Picture Library/Getty Images; p. 14 Josephine Julian/Shutterstock.com; p. 17 © Look and Learn/Bridgeman Images; p. 18 benoitb/DigitalVision Vectors/Getty Images; p. 21 Library of Congress, Geography and Map Division; p. 22 New York Public Library/Science Source; p. 25 My Portfolio/Shutterstock.com; p. 26 DEA Picture Library/De Agostini/Getty Images; p. 29 Godong/Universal Images Group/Getty Images; p. 30 DEA/A. Dagli Orti/De Agostini Picture Library/Getty Images; p. 33 JLGutierrez/E+/Getty Images; p. 34 Division of Medicine and Science, National Museum of American History, Smithsonian Institution; p. 37 neenawat khenyothaa/Shutterstock.com; p. 38 Jwilliamlee/Shutterstock.com; p. 41 StunningArt/Shutterstock.com; p. 42 Chaay_Tee/Shutterstock.com; cover and interior pages background pattern Sylfida/Shutterstock.com.

Some of the images in this book illustrate individuals who are models. The depictions do not imply actual situations or events.

Cataloging-in-Publication Data

Names: Fitch, Kevin.
Title: The Chinese invent the compass / Kevin Fitch.
Description: New York : Rosen Publishing, 2022. | Series: Crazy cool China | Includes glossary and index.
Identifiers: ISBN 9781499469158 (pbk.) | ISBN 9781499469165 (library bound) | ISBN 9781499469172 (ebook)
Subjects: LCSH: Technology—China—History—Juvenile literature. | Science—China—History—Juvenile literature. | Inventions—China—History—Juvenile literature.
Classification: LCC T27.C5 F583 2022 | DDC 609.31—dc23

*Manufactured in the United States of America*

CPSIA Compliance Information: Batch #BSRYA22. For further information contact Rosen Publishing, New York, New York at 1-800-237-9932.

# Contents

# The Compass: One of the "Four Great Inventions" of China

Imagine what it would be like to live in a world in which you could never wander more than a few miles from your home and some important landmarks that **oriented** you. Imagine what it would be like if most ships had to stay within a few miles of shore and could not **navigate** on cloudy or foggy days. Imagine a world without reliable maps or sea charts, and with no Global Positioning System (GPS) to help you feel confident that you always knew exactly where you were, where you had come from, and where you were going. This was, in fact, the world that existed before the invention of the compass.

As with so many of the world's most transformative inventions, the inventors were not seeking to create the tool that ultimately resulted and that we now celebrate. The compass might have been first developed to serve as an aid to fortune-telling and to assist in practicing the art of **feng shui**. Before long, however, its utility as a tool for orienteering on land and navigating at sea became apparent.

We have China to thank for the invention of the compass, by some accounts over 2,500 years ago. The discovery of how to reliably determine direction and orient oneself in space was so momentous and had so many revolutionary technological, scientific, historical, cultural, and economic ripple effects that the compass is considered one of the "Four Great Inventions" of China (along with gunpowder, papermaking, and printing).

This Song Dynasty (960–1279 CE) compass was discovered in 1973 at the site of a thirteenth-century shipwreck off the coast of Quanzhou, in Fujian Province. When filled with water, the head of the magnetic fish would point south, and its tail would point north.

18:54
Search places
0,2
150

With the invention of the compass, distant lands could now be discovered and mapped. Sea voyages could extend far from shore. Ships could sail in foggy and cloudy conditions and starless nights. As a result, exploration and trade exploded. Once separated cultures began to trade goods, technology, ideas, literature, and even religion among each other. Long-separated civilizations came into greater communication with each other, becoming mutually enriched in the process.

Even today, the compass continues to be central to **orienteering**, seafaring, and aviation, and has many military and even religious applications. Directly and indirectly, it has led to many of the modern era's navigational and directional tools, like reliable maps and marine charts, **longitude** and **latitude**, radio navigation systems and radar, electromagnetism and electronic communications, **gyroscopes**, GPS, and smartphone map apps. So the next time you are lost in a strange city and using your phone to help guide you to a familiar place, thank the Chinese for their gift of the compass that made it all possible!

While compasses have been replaced for many people by GPS and map apps, the wireless technology that modern direction-finding relies upon evolved from the ancient discovery of the compass and electromagnetism.

# Navigation Before the Compass

Before the invention of the compass and its use as a navigational tool sometime around the tenth or eleventh century CE, traveling the world's oceans was far more difficult and dangerous. Most early **mariners** traveled fairly close to the coastline, determining their course and identifying their direction by sighting landmarks along the shore.

Over time, sailors developed other means of determining location and direction. The sun and stars were particularly useful for helping to identify one's location and plot a

In addition to celestial navigation, sailors used other methods to determine location and direction. The temperature of wind could be "read." A cold wind typically came from the north, a warm damp wind from the south. Eight kinds of winds were identified and associated with particular directions. Sailors also released birds, and if the birds did not return to the ship, they would follow the direction the birds took, assuming that land was nearby.

course to one's desired destination. The most basic examples include identifying east and west based upon where the sun rises and sets, and north and south can be determined by the directions of shadows cast by the sun at high noon. The stars also rise in the east at nighttime and set in the west before dawn. And, in the Northern Hemisphere, the star Polaris, also known as the North Star, is nearly aligned with Earth's northern axis and therefore "points" north.

Measuring the angles between the sun, moon, planets, or stars and the horizon line allowed sailors to locate their position on the ocean, even when far from

This Chinese star chart from around 700 CE is the earliest surviving atlas of the night sky and shows over 1,300 stars. It is based on observations made by three Chinese astronomers more than a thousand years earlier, long before the seventeenth-century invention of the telescope.

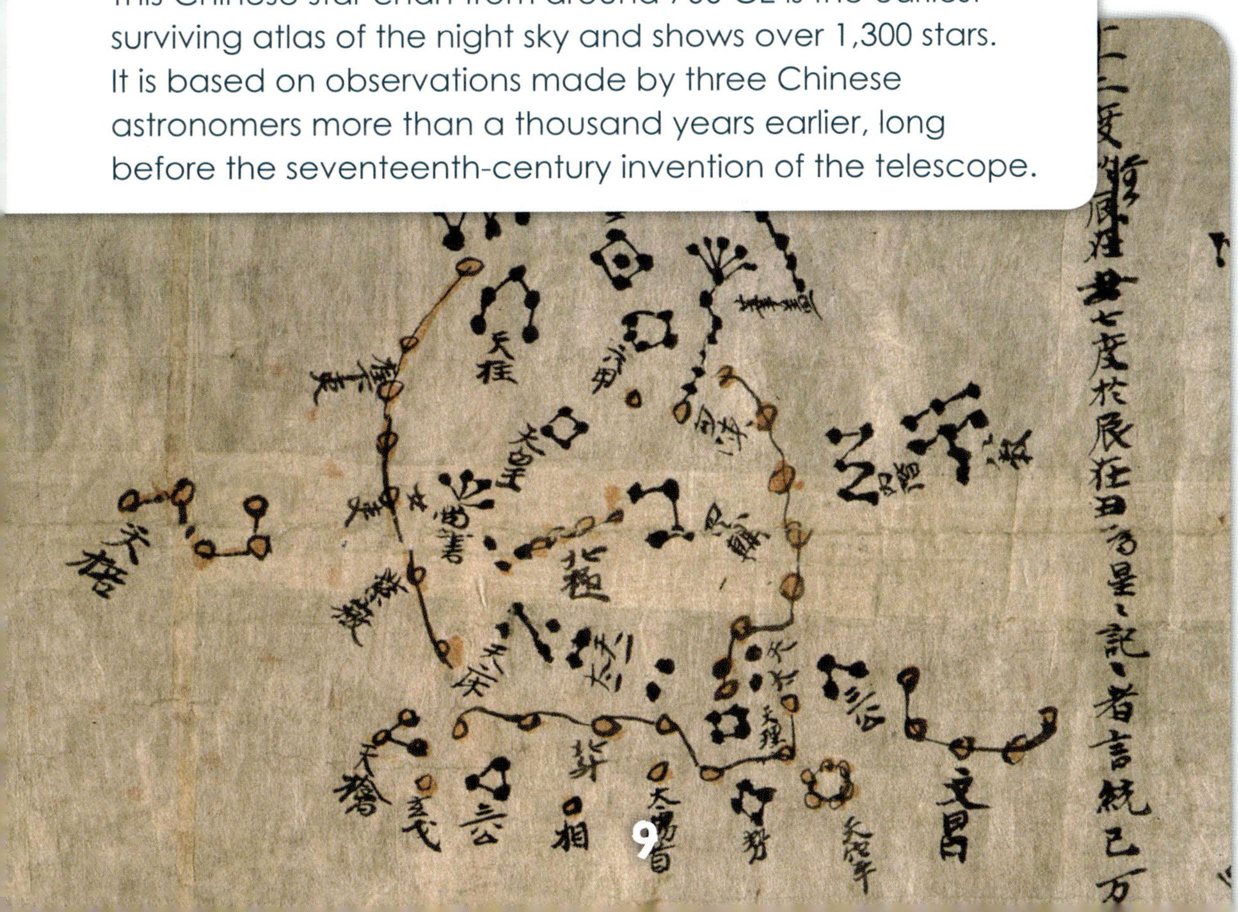

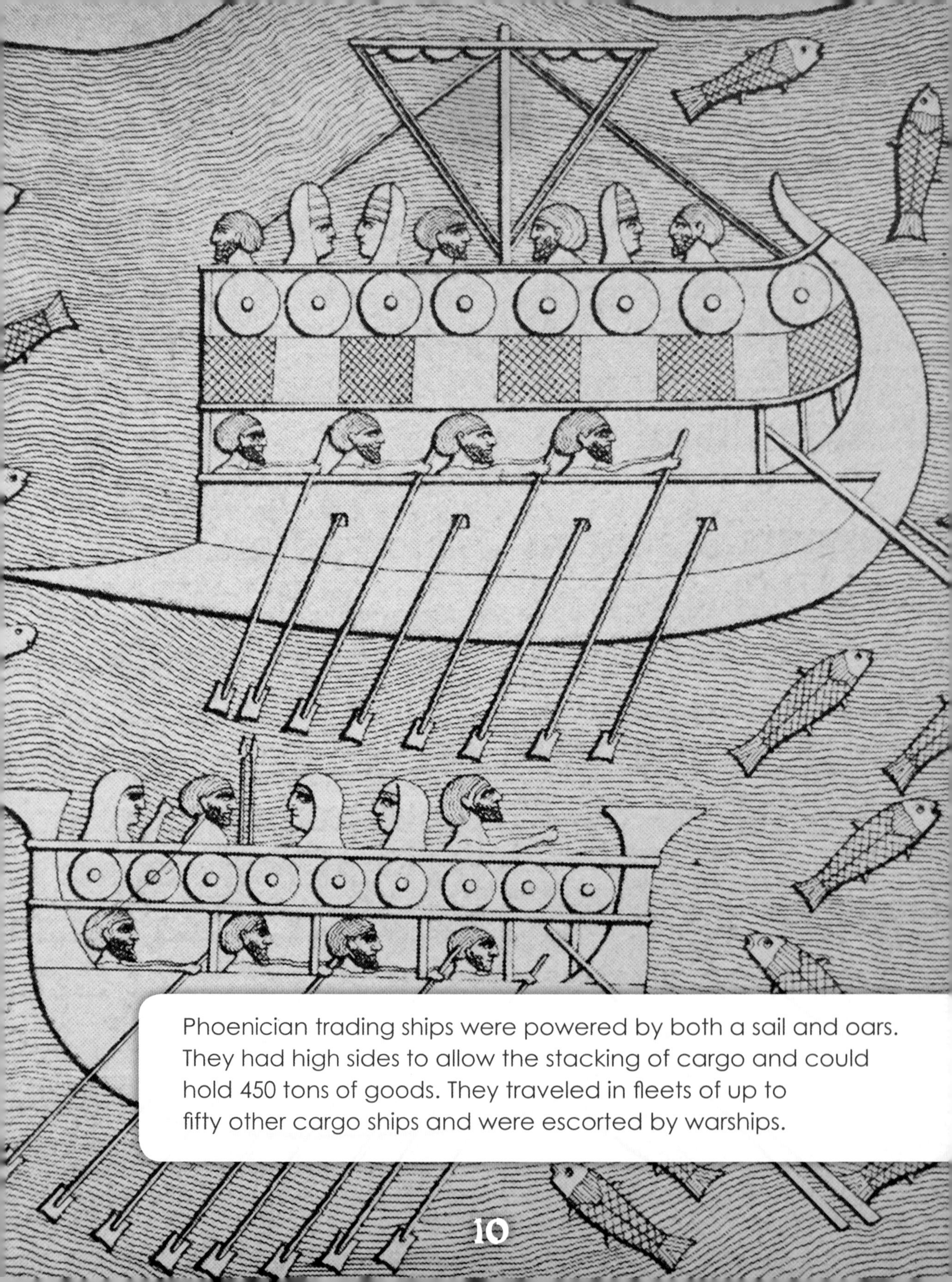

Phoenician trading ships were powered by both a sail and oars. They had high sides to allow the stacking of cargo and could hold 450 tons of goods. They traveled in fleets of up to fifty other cargo ships and were escorted by warships.

The manner in which sea debris drifted could help ancient sailors identify currents, which, in turn, gave them clues as to their ship's location and direction. Both Viking and Chinese mariners studied sea floor mud, whose color and texture gave them clues about their present location. Vikings also used crystals that **polarized** the sunlight and allowed them to determine the sun's direction and elevation, even on cloudy and foggy days.

land. This was known as **celestial** navigation, and it allowed sea voyages to extend farther. One of the earliest long distance sea routes was the course taken between Crete and Egypt by trading ships beginning around 2500 BCE. In the seventh century BCE, Phoenician traders were sailing to the southwest coast of England. Fourth and fifth century CE Polynesian ships sailed more than 2,000 miles (3,220 km) to reach Hawaii. And the Vikings are now widely believed to have sailed to North America repeatedly beginning in the tenth century CE.

These longer sea voyages allowed for an increase in trade, exploration, communication, and cultural exchange. With the introduction of the compass, this early form of globalization would accelerate even more rapidly and usher the world into the modern era.

# Fortune-Telling and Feng Shui

As early as the fourth century BCE, the Chinese discovered that lodestone, a form of the rock mineral magnetite, is naturally magnetized. Magnets align themselves with Earth's magnetic field and, if largely free of gravity and friction, will always point to Earth's magnetic poles. Magnetism may have seemed magical to the Chinese. As a result, they incorporated lodestone into their **divination** and fortune-telling practices.

> The eight **trigrams** of the *I Ching* represent heaven, lake, fire, thunder, wind, water, mountain, and earth. Two trigrams are randomly combined through a sort of game of chance—by throwing sticks or coins, for example. The resulting hexagram has a stable and established meaning that indicates a certain fortune or prediction, such as stagnation, peace, splitting apart, turning point, or abundance.

The first compass invented by the Chinese, perhaps around 200 BCE, was not a compass at all as we would now define it. It was not designed as a navigation aid but rather as a tool for **geomancy** and was known as a diviner's board. The "needle" of the compass, was a lodestone that was spoon-shaped. It was placed on a bronze plate upon which were inscribed four **cardinal directions** and the eight trigrams of the *I Ching* (an ancient divination text), as well as twenty-four directions (corresponding to constellations) and twenty-four lunar "houses" (corresponding to constellations that divide the equator). The Big Dipper often appeared on a disc at the center of the board, where the lodestone would sit. The handle of the lodestone always pointed south, as the bowl of the "spoon" pointed north. This is why the Chinese word for compass is "south-pointing needle." The disc represented heaven, while the square board signified Earth.

This is a Chinese geomantic compass, used for the purposes of divination and feng shui. Its direction-locating abilities would allow builders to find just the right site and positioning for houses, graves, and other structures to ensure harmony with the forces around them and the good fortune of those who would inhabit them.

Feng shui is a form of geomancy that seeks to use free-flowing energy to harmonize individuals with nature and their environment. Traditional practice sought to use feng shui—and the compass, its most important tool—to orient buildings in the most harmonious, balanced, and **auspicious** manner possible. Human structures—such as temples, tombs, and private dwellings—should be built on locations with good *qi*, or energy, that is not blocked in any way.

By interpreting the lines and geometric alignments indicated by the pointing lodestone, diviners felt they were able to predict likely shifts of fortune and determine the best times for certain activities, such as funerals. The diviner's board pinpointed where and when certain crops would best be planted and where precious gems might be found. Following the principles of feng shui and using the cardinal directions, the "south-pointing needle" was also used to plot the most harmonious alignment of new buildings, houses, temples, and even gravesites.

Compasses are still used in traditional feng shui practices. Unlike the typical compass seen at left, a compass used for feng shui is called a *luopan*, and its needle points to magnetic south. It has markings for twenty-four directions and can have as many as forty concentric rings around it containing feng shui formulas.

# South-Pointing Fish and Mysterious Needles

The first mention of magnetism in Chinese writings occurs in a fourth-century-BCE collection of political texts that notes that lodestones attract iron. The same collection of writings mentions that people in the central Chinese state of Zheng determine their position in space with the use of a "south-pointer." The first mention of a lodestone "spoon" pointing in a cardinal direction—rather than being used strictly for fortune-telling or feng shui purposes—is found in a classic Chinese text known as the *Lunheng* (c. 70–80 CE), which is devoted to natural sciences,

Two ninth-century-CE texts provide evidence that the Chinese discovered the principle of magnetic declination. This is the angle on the horizontal plane between **magnetic north** and **true north**. The angle varies depending on where you are standing on Earth's surface, and it can change at that location over time. A compass is needed to calculate magnetic declination, so China's "south pointer" must have been used as a proper compass by this time.

mythology, philosophy, and literature. The author describes a spoon being thrown to the ground and coming to a rest pointing south.

It would not be until much later—the early eleventh century CE—that the first explicit mention of the "south-pointer" being used as a direction finder for navigating land would be made. A military reference book dated to 1040–1044 CE, known as the *Wujing Zongyao* ("Collection of the Most Important Military Techniques"), describes an iron "south-pointing fish" that floats in a bowl of water. Its unvarying ability to always point south made it a useful tool for journeying over land in darkness or when bad weather made visibility poor: "When troops encountered gloomy weather or dark nights, and the directions of space could not be distinguished...they made use of the... south-pointing fish."

Chinese scholars use a diviner's board to help determine the future and identify the most harmonious placement for planned structures, such as homes and graves.

With a "wet" compass, a magnetized needle would be attached to a wooden splinter or cork and floated in a bowl of water. Some felt the water made the needle too unsteady, however. So they instead attached the needle to a suspended piece of silk and allowed it to float freely in the air. This was known as a suspended compass and could only be used in windless weather to ensure an accurate indication of north-south.

The reference to a "south-pointing fish" rather than a "south-pointing spoon" may indicate that the lodestone spoon of the diviner's board and the "south-pointer" had been replaced by an iron needle whose tip had been rubbed by a lodestone, thus magnetizing it. Indeed, a "mysterious needle" that is magnetic and shaped like a tadpole is mentioned in a tenth-century Chinese text. The actual process of magnetizing a direction-finding needle with a lodestone is described in the *Dream Pool Essays*, written by the former statesman and general Shen Kuo in 1088.

This Chinese text, written by the eleventh-century-CE scientist, statesman, and general Shen Kuo, describes four different ways to install a compass's magnetized needle. He was the first person ever to discuss artificial magnetization.

# The Compass Sets Sail

China's development of the wet compass was a great improvement over the bulky and heavy diviner's board used for the purposes of geomancy and feng shui. The wet compass was comparatively light and portable. It was these advantages that probably first encouraged Chinese mariners to bring the compasses aboard their ships.

Detailed compass readings taken during famed Chinese navigator Zheng He's military and trade expeditions led to the creation of a set of navigation charts known collectively as the Zheng He Navigation Map. Dated to about 1422, it is the earliest set of maps to offer somewhat accurate representations of Southern Asia, Persia, Arabia, and East Africa. The chart mainly maps coastal regions—inland areas are much less accurate—and includes sailing routes and sailing instructions.

Just over sixty-five years after the first reference to Chinese use of the compass for land navigation, we see the first mention of its use for maritime navigation. In the

c. 1111–1117 CE book *Pingzhou Table Talks*, written by the Song-era historian Zhu Yu, the author describes mariners using a combination of landmark identification, celestial navigation, and the compass to pilot their ships. He makes the use of the compass sound like an ordinary and unremarkable activity, indicating it may have already been used for maritime navigation for some time: “The ship’s pilots are acquainted with the configuration of the coasts; at night, they steer by stars and, in the daytime, by the sun. In dark weather, they look at the south-pointing needle.”

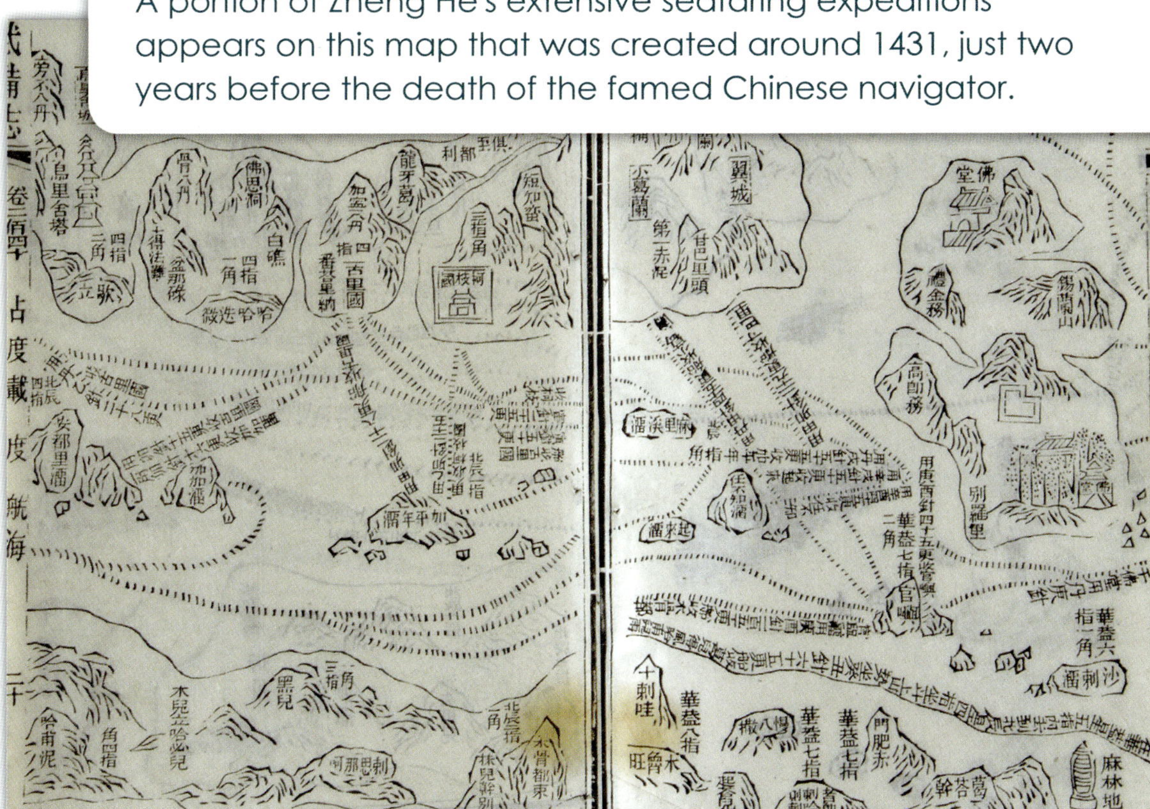


A portion of Zheng He's extensive seafaring expeditions appears on this map that was created around 1431, just two years before the death of the famed Chinese navigator.

A Song Dynasty (960–1279 CE) suspended compass appears below. This type of compass could be used only in windless conditions and was therefore not useful as a shipboard navigation device.

The Chinese dry compass featured a wooden frame shaped like a turtle. It contained a lodestone, sealed to a pivot by wax. This dry-mounted needle was the turtle's "tail," and it would point north. Dry compasses would begin to appear in Europe by around 1300 CE and became very popular. Though China's dry compass was used into the eighteenth century, Chinese sailors preferred the wet compass for hundreds of years.

The relative lack of gravity and friction exerted on the magnetized needle in both a wet compass and a suspended compass allowed it to reliably point north-south. Yet a suspended compass was impractical on a ship, as there were seldom windless conditions, especially when the ship was under sail. The wet compass had some drawbacks, too. The wood or cork that the needle was attached to often bobbed in the water, making it hard to "read" and making the north-south designation less accurate and definite. Wet compasses could also leak and be difficult to repair. Possibly in response to the limitations of wet and suspended compasses, the Chinese developed a dry compass in the early twelfth century, about 200 years before they first appeared in Europe.

# China Offers the Compass to the World

With the onboard navigation system provided by the compass, Chinese ships were able to venture farther from home shores. Indeed, there is evidence to suggest that Chinese mariners were able to sail as far as Saudi Arabia without getting lost. Trade and communication with distant lands increased in both volume and speed. In this way, the sea routes associated with the Silk Road became both more extensive and expansive. The Silk Road was a network of trade routes—both land and sea—that wound throughout Asia, the Middle East, Africa, and

> In his *De utensilibus* ("On Instruments," c. 1187), English scholar Alexander Neckam declares, "If then one wishes a ship well provided with all things, then one must have also a needle mounted on a dart. The needle will be oscillated and turn until the point of the needle directs itself to [North], thus making known to sailors the route which they should hold."

Southern Europe. It is named for the Chinese silk that was its most important trade good.

Inevitably, with this increase in trade and communication, knowledge of the compass spread to the ports visited by Chinese ships. It was not just trade goods that traveled the Silk Road. Ideas, philosophies, religion, and technology all began circulating throughout Europe, Africa, the Middle East, and Asia. The Silk Road is believed to have played a significant part in the spread of the other three "Great Inventions" of China—papermaking, printing, and gunpowder.

The map shows various trade routes associated with the Silk Road travel and trade network.

European mariners are shown consulting an onboard compass to determine direction and maintain course in this medieval-era illustration.

In his *De naturis rerum* ("On the Nature of Things," c. 1190), Neckham reported that "when in cloudy weather...or when the world is wrapped up in the darkness of the shades of night, and [the sailors] are ignorant to what point of the compass their ship's course is directed, they touch the magnet with a needle, which is whirled round in a circle until its point looks direct to the north."

It remains unclear exactly how knowledge of the compass spread throughout Europe and the Muslim world. Most historians believe some combination of the Silk Road, the travels of Western Crusaders and pilgrims to the Holy Land, and the greater reach and speed of Chinese maritime trade introduced compass technology to the rest of the world and allowed its use to spread quickly. Others, however, believe that the compass was developed in Europe and China more or less simultaneously and independent of each other.

What is known is that the first mention of the compass in the West occurs in the work of the English scholar and abbot Alexander Neckam, around 1190 CE, about eighty years after the first Chinese account of its use on ships.

# The Compass Launches the Age of Discovery

By the early thirteenth century CE, the compass was being used as a maritime navigational instrument in Europe, India, the Muslim world, and parts of eastern Africa. These early compasses—featuring magnetized needles floating in a bowl of water—are very similar to Chinese designs, possibly arguing in favor of a Chinese origin for their adoption of the technology. Persian and Indian descriptions of a fish-shaped iron pointer are strong echoes of the Chinese "south-pointing fish."

In addition to its use as a maritime navigational tool, Muslims embraced the compass for its more spiritual utility. As early as the thirteenth century, the compass was being used as a qibla indicator. Qibla is the direction in which Muslims should face when offering their prayers. They should be pointing toward the Kaaba, considered the House of God, within the Great Mosque of Mecca, in Saudi Arabia.

The compass allowed European sailors to travel between the Mediterranean and Northern Europe, even as far as the English Channel. Muslim sailors plied the waters of the Red Sea and the Persian Gulf. Voyages could now be undertaken in some of the winter months and in weather that once kept ships in port. Trade, cultural, and political contacts increased, as did conflict. European nations adopted the compass enthusiastically, in part, in order to gain military and economic advantage over their rivals. This helped to usher in the Age of Discovery of the fifteenth to eighteenth centuries.

The ships of England, Spain, Portugal, and the Netherlands were soon crisscrossing the globe, "discovering" and exploring the New World, founding

The user of this iPad has downloaded a qibla app in order to determine the location of Mecca and the direction in which to offer daily prayers.

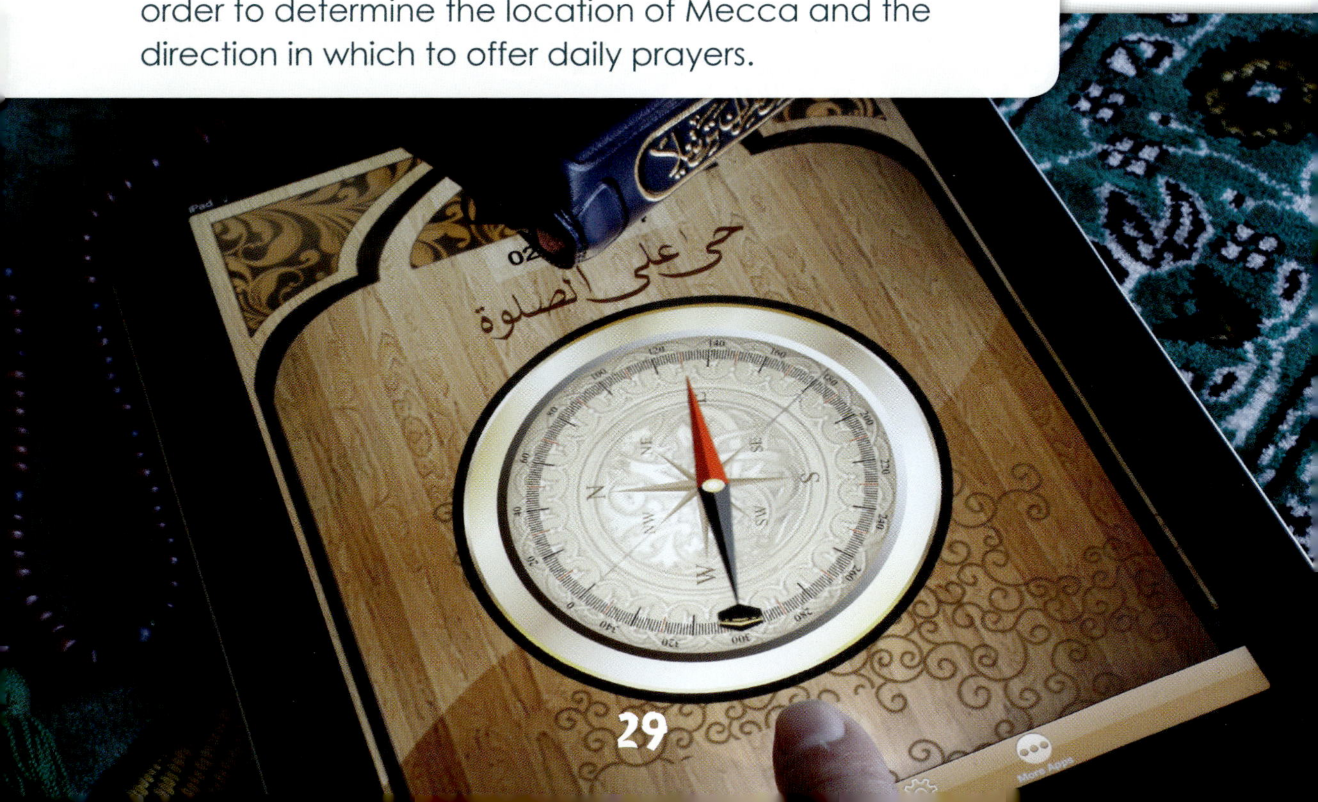

The Mediterranean coastal regions of Europe, North Africa, Asia Minor, and the Middle East are mapped in great detail and with accuracy in this sixteenth-century nautical chart made by a mapmaker from Venice, Italy.

Nautical charts based upon compass readings began to be created in the thirteenth century. They could not provide reliable open ocean sailing instructions but instead offered accurate depictions of smaller bodies of water, like the Mediterranean, Black, and Red Seas. These charts included lists of ports, coastal landmarks, and distances. Eventually, similar charts were drawn up for parts of the Atlantic and Pacific and the newly discovered seas of Africa, the Americas, and South Asia.

colonies, extracting wealth, and waging war on the high seas. Explorers, navigators, and merchants charted new sea routes to the Far East, opening up additional opportunities for trade in spices, tea, and silk. Spanish conquistadores invaded and plundered Central and South America, exploiting its wealth of natural resources. The governments of France, Spain, England, and the Netherlands created new colonies in Africa and on the far side of the Atlantic Ocean.

The compass had utterly transformed the world, our ability to move through it, and our capacity to know it. Yet indirectly, the compass also brought great suffering, as European explorers and colonists **decimated** the **indigenous** civilizations and peoples of the Americas and enslaved millions of Africans.

# Improving the Compass

Because of the importance of seafaring to their economic might and political power, European nations embraced the compass and came to rely heavily upon it. For this reason, improvements to the compass were made primarily by Europeans, especially the English.

In 1862, a new wet compass was developed that allowed the card to float, taking weight off of the easily broken pivot upon which the needle was mounted. The tendency to leak was also corrected by creating a bellows system that accommodates changes in the volume of liquid caused by shifts in temperature. At this point, the new and improved wet compass became the standard for most world navies, and dry card compasses began to disappear.

Early European compasses were composed of bowls filled with water and a magnetized needle mounted on a pivot or pin that stood on the bottom of the bowl. Early compasses had only two directions that appeared on the bowl—north and south. Eventually, a card was placed under the needle that indicated thirty-two directions—the four cardinal directions (north, south, east, and west) and twenty-eight inter-cardinal points (such as north-by-west, north-north-west, north-west-by-north, northwest, northwest-by-west, west-northwest, and west-by-north). The card would turn as the ship changed direction, while the needle remained pointing north. This innovation allowed mariners to determine their precise direction simply by glancing at the card.

Because the wet compass was heavy, often leaked, and had a delicate pivot that broke easily and was hard to fix, Europeans, like the Chinese before them, developed dry compasses. The water in the bowl helped to absorb the shocks of the ship's motion and keep the

The compasses below feature various kinds of compass cards that mark the thirty-two cardinal and inter-cardinal directions. Compass cards, also known as compass roses or wind roses, could be very decorative and beautiful, as well as highly practical aids to direction finding.

This nineteenth-century dry card compass sits within a wooden bowl that is suspended on a gimbal and sits within a wooden box. It had the advantage over wet card compasses of being lighter and less likely to break or leak.

To correct for declination, some European compass makers mounted the magnetic needle slightly askew so that it pointed to magnetic north while a marking on the card indicated true north. However, this solution only worked for short voyages that did not venture far from where the compass was made. Because the angle of declination changes from location to location and also varies over time, any long-lasting and distant voyage would be subject to directional inaccuracy and straying from charted courses.

compass needle level, ensuring accurate readings. Dry card compasses had to achieve this stability differently. The needle would be suspended over the compass card and pivot freely on a pin. In addition, the case containing the needle, pin, and compass card were suspended on rings called gimbals, which allowed the compass to swing freely and stay level, not shifting and tilting with the ship's motion.

The Chinese had discovered the principle of declination—the difference in angle between true north and magnetic north—in the ninth century CE. The difference is least at the equator and greater closer to the poles. Fifteenth-century European explorers and navigators—including Christopher Columbus—began noticing this discrepancy and making adjustments to the compass and its readings to help prevent them from being led hundreds of miles off course.

# Modern Compasses

Modern compasses come in various types with many features. Most of them are light and handheld and include a magnetized needle or dial sealed within a liquid-filled container. The liquid helps keep the needle steady and stable, allowing for more accurate and quickly determined direction readings.

Once the Age of Sail yielded to the Age of Steam in the second half of the nineteenth century, onboard compasses had to adapt to new iron- and steel-hulled ships. The magnetism of the metal ships could throw off the compass readings, making them inaccurate. One solution was to place soft iron balls and bar magnets near the compass to help correct the compass's readings.

Orienteering compasses (for land navigation) usually include a box that allows the user to align the needle with magnetic north. The compass's base features orienting lines and a direction-of-travel indicator. This base is transparent, so it can be laid over maps in order to plot positions and measure distances. An outer dial displays degree markings. Many military and orienteering compasses include sights or viewfinders that allow you to read the bearings and angles off of the compass card while at the same time aligning the compass with a desired object in the distance. The compass's dial and markings may be illuminated through the use of phosphorescent or even radioactive materials.

This military-style orienteering compass includes an optical viewfinder that allows the user to align the compass with objects in the distance while still being able to read the bearings on the compass dial.

The compass remains important to modern navigation of roadways, seaways, and airways. A compass is one of the crucial instruments on the flight deck of modern airplanes, along with altimeters, turn coordinators, and indicators of air speed, vertical speed, and heading.

Another solution to the problem of the magnetism of metal ships throwing off a compass's readings was the gyrocompass. This is a non-magnetic compass that always indicates true north with the help of a continuously spinning gyroscope whose axis is parallel to Earth's axis of rotation. Not only is a gyroscope unaffected by the magnetism of ship metal, it also points to true north, not magnetic north, thereby eliminating the problem of declination.

Modern mariners' compasses are mounted on cylindrical pedestals known as binnacles. Magnets are placed within the binnacle to counteract the magnetism of the ship's metal. A marking known as a lubber line appears on the compass bowl and indicates the ship's heading on the compass card. The compass's face is illuminated from within the binnacle.

Airplanes use a compass very similar to that found in modern ships. It is known as a gyromagnetic compass, and it, too, is mounted in a binnacle that corrects for the magnetism of the plane's metal skin. Yet there is another factor that can disrupt the accuracy of an airplane's compass readings—sudden changes in direction. So an airplane's compass includes a gyroscope whose axis of spin is not altered by changes in the plane's direction. As a result, the compass readings remain accurate throughout the entire flight.

# Celebrate China!

It was the discovery of magnetism that first allowed the Chinese to develop the compass. The study of magnetism eventually led to a greater understanding of electromagnetism, which resulted in inventions like electric power generation, the electric motor, and electronic communications, including the telegraph and telephone. Magnetism even influenced wireless telecommunications, via radio waves, a form of

The compass greatly increased the movement of people, goods, and ideas around the globe. Knowledge was spread and shared, technology advanced, and scientific discoveries were made at an accelerating pace. The concepts of longitude and latitude were developed, as were useful instruments like the **chronometer**. As a result, mapping of the world and its oceans became far more detailed and accurate, and seafaring became far more safe, efficient, and **lucrative**.

electromagnetic radiation. Communication satellite technology is based upon the relay of radio signals, as are the locating and detecting abilities of radar.

The magnetic compass is also the origin of one of the modern era's greatest forms of location technology—the Global Positioning System (GPS). This is a satellite-based radio navigation system that can provide anyone with a GPS receiver (such as a smartphone GPS app or a dedicated GPS receiver in the car) with location information, almost anywhere they may be in the world. The user's receiver is in communication with at least four GPS satellites, each of which transmits radio signals

In our digital age, compasses may seem like a relic of the pre-modern era. But there would be no GPS or wireless technology without the scientific discoveries and explorations begun with and made possible by the compass.

Today, we can communicate with entire groups of friends and family across the world, thanks to wireless and satellite technology. The magnetic compass helped make this possible, both directly and indirectly. As a tool that encouraged exploration, discovery, and cultural exchange, it was one of the world's first great global communication devices.

China began using the compass for maritime navigation almost 1,000 years ago, most likely before any other seafaring nation. And China remains one of the world's leading naval powers and design innovators, even as it continues to modernize its fleet. A recent US Defense Intelligence Agency report states, "China's technological advancement in naval design has begun to approach a level commensurate with, and in some cases exceeding, that of other modern navies."

containing time and current location information. The GPS receiver then calculates its own location relative to these satellites using latitude, longitude, and height coordinates. GPS receivers can pinpoint the user's location to within about 1 foot (30 cm).

GPS represents just the latest technology to have been built upon the foundation created by the Chinese discovery of the compass. As an instrument that has been used to create harmony and good fortune, map land and sea, provide direction, promote exploration and discovery, create connections among the nations of the world, and facilitate the spread of ideas and technology and culture, the compass is far more than just a direction finder. It is perhaps the world's greatest communication device, one that has inspired us to look outward, beyond ourselves, to venture forth into the great world beyond and greet our fellow travelers. For this, we owe China an enormous debt of gratitude!

# Glossary

**auspicious** Showing or suggesting that future success is likely.

**cardinal direction** One of the four main directions—North, East, South, and West—usually appearing on a compass as N, E, S, and W.

**celestial** Relating to the sky and the visible heavens.

**chronometer** A timepiece designed to keep accurate time from the home port to the destination despite the negative effects of outside forces, like magnetism, air pressure, temperature, humidity, and the pitch and roll of the ship.

**decimate** To destroy or significantly harm; drastically reduce in size or number.

**divination** The practice of trying to tell fortunes, predict future events, or discover hidden knowledge.

**feng shui** A Chinese geomantic, or geographical divination, practice in which a structure or site is chosen or configured in such a way as to harmonize with the spiritual forces inhabiting and surrounding it.

**geomancy** Divination using figures, lines, or geographic features.

**gyroscope** A wheel that spins quickly and is held in a frame that allows its axis to tilt and spin in any direction.

**indigenous** Produced, growing, living, or occurring natively or naturally in a particular region or environment.

**latitude** Angular distance north or south from Earth's equator measured in degrees up to 90 degrees and running parallel to the equator.

**longitude** Distance measured in degrees east or west from an imaginary line called the prime meridian, which goes from the North Pole to the South Pole, passing through Greenwich, England.

**lucrative** Producing wealth; profitable.

**magnetic north** The northerly direction in Earth's magnetic field indicated by the north-seeking pole of a compass needle.

**mariner** Sailer; seafarer.

**navigate** To travel by water; to sail; to steer a course through a medium, like air, water, or a highway system.

**orient** To situate in space; to be made aware of one's location in space.

**orienteering** An activity in which one uses a map and compass to navigate between checkpoints along and throughout unfamiliar terrain (like a forest).

**polarize** To cause light waves to vibrate in a certain pattern in one direction or within a single plane. When light is reflected by shiny or transparent materials, like water, asphalt, or other nonmetallic surfaces, it becomes polarized—the reflected light is vibrating in one direction. Examples of polarized light include glare, the blue sky, and rainbows. Polarized light is used in imaging technology to create sharper images. Sunglasses can be polarized to reduce glare.

**trigram** One of the eight possible combinations of three whole or broken lines used in Chinese divination practices.

**true north** North that is calculated by plotting an imaginary line through Earth, from pole to pole; the direction that leads to the North Pole.

# For More Information

**Asia Society** (three locations)
725 Park Avenue
New York, NY 10021
(212) 288-6400

1370 Southmore Boulevard
Houston, TX 77004

9 Justice Drive
Admiralty Hong Kong
852-2103-9511
Website: https://asiasociety.org
Asia Society is the leading educational organization dedicated to promoting mutual understanding and strengthening partnerships among people, leaders, and institutions of Asia and the United States in a global context.

**China Maritime Museum**
197 Shengang Avenue
Lingang New City
Pudong New District
Shanghai, China 201306
86-021-38287777
Website: http://www.shmmc.com.cn/English/index
The China Maritime Museum is the first national maritime museum approved by the State Council of the People's Republic of China and jointly built by the Ministry of Transport of China and Shanghai Municipal People's Government. It features the largest collection of its kind in the country, with a focus on navigation and historical relics. The museum is composed of six exhibition halls, two special exhibition areas, two science movie theaters, and a children's amusement center.

**Chinese Historical Society of America**
965 Clay Street
San Francisco, CA 94108
(415) 391-1188, ext. 101
Website: https://chsa.org
The Chinese Historical Society of America Museum is the oldest organization in the country dedicated to the interpretation, promotion, and preservation of the social, cultural, and political history and contributions of the Chinese in America.

**Museum of Chinese in America**
215 Centre Street
New York, NY 10013
(855) 955-MOCA
Website: http://www.mocanyc.org
Founded in 1980, the Museum of Chinese in America (MOCA) is dedicated to preserving and presenting the history, heritage, culture, and diverse experiences of people of Chinese descent in the United States.

**Museum of Maritime Navigation and Communication**
1208 Bay Street
Staten Island, NY 10305
(718) 594-1717
Website: http://mmncny.org
The Museum of Maritime Navigation and Communication is dedicated to the preservation of marine electronic equipment and maritime history.

**Museum of Science and Industry, Chicago**
5700 South Lake Shore
Chicago, IL 60637
(773) 684-1414
Website: https://www.msichicago.org
The Museum of Science and Industry, Chicago—one of the largest science museums in the world—is home to more than 400,000 square feet (37,000 sq m) of hands-on exhibits designed to spark scientific inquiry and creativity.

**Mystic Seaport Museum**
75 Greenmanville Avenue
Mystic, CT 06355
(860) 572-0711
Website: https://www.mysticseaport.org
Mystic Seaport Museum is one of the world's leading maritime museums. Founded in 1929 to preserve the rapidly disappearing artifacts of our seafaring past, the museum has become a national center for research and education with the mission to inspire an enduring connection to the maritime experience. The museum's grounds cover 19 acres (8 ha) on the Mystic River in Mystic, Conn., and include a re-created New England coastal village, a working shipyard, exhibit halls, and state-of-the-art artifact storage facilities. The museum is home to more than 500 historic watercraft.

**National Museum of China (NMC)**
No. 16 East Chang'an Street
Dongcheng District
Beijing, China 100006
Website: http://en.chnmuseum.cn
The NMC is a palace of history and art reflecting and displaying China's traditional and modern culture. It houses more than 1.4 million objects that typify and bear witness to the richness and depth of China's 5,000-year-old civilization.

# For Further Reading


Abulafia, David. *The Boundless Sea: A Human History of the Oceans*. New York, NY: Oxford University Press, 2019.

Abulafia, David. *The Great Sea: A Human History of the Mediterranean*. New York, NY: Oxford University Press, 2013.

Bardoe, Cheryl, and the Field Museum. *China: A History*. New York, NY: Harry N. Abrams, 2019.

Blake, John. *The Sea Chart: The Illustrated History of Nautical Maps and Navigational Charts*. London, UK: Conway Maritime Press, 2016.

Brotton, Jerry. *A History of the World in 12 Maps*. New York, NY: Penguin Books, 2014.

Cotterell, Arthur. *Ancient China*. New York, NY: DK Eyewitness, 2005.

Culp, Jennifer. *Ancient Chinese Technology*. New York, NY: Rosen Publishing, 2016.

Dixon, Chris, and Jeremy K. Spencer. *Ocean: The Ultimate Handbook of Nautical Knowledge*. San Francisco, CA: Chronicle Books, 2020.

Frankopan, Peter. *The Silk Roads: A New History of the World*. New York, NY: Bloomsbury Publishing, 2015.

Hanson-Harding, Brian. *Ancient Chinese Religion and Beliefs*. New York, NY: Rosen Publishing, 2016.

Harrison-Hall, Jessica. *China: A History in Objects*. London, UK: Thames & Hudson, 2018.

Liu, Jing. *Barbarians and the Birth of Chinese Identity: The Five Dynasties and Ten Kingdoms to the Yuan Dynasty (907–1368)* (Understanding China Through Comics). Berkeley, CA: Stone Bridge Press, 2017.

Liu, Jing. *Division to Unification in Imperial China: The Three Kingdoms to the Tang Dynasty (220–907)* (Understanding China Through Comics). Berkeley, CA: Stone Bridge Press, 2016.

Liu, Jing. *Foundations of Chinese Civilization: The Yellow Emperor to the Han Dynasty (2697 BCE–220 CE)* (Understanding China Through Comics). Berkeley, CA: Stone Bridge Press, 2016.

Liu, Jing. *The Making of Modern China: The Ming Dynasty to the Qing Dynasty (1368–1912)* (Understanding China Through Comics). Berkeley, CA: Stone Bridge Press, 2017.

Lusted, Marcia Amidon. *Ancient Chinese Daily Life*. New York, NY: Rosen Publishing, 2016.

Morrow, Paula. *Ancient Chinese Culture*. New York, NY: Rosen Publishing, 2016.

Paine, Lincoln. *The Sea & Civilization: A Maritime History of the World*. New York, NY: Vintage, 2015.

# Bibliography


Abulafia, David. *The Boundless Sea: A Human History of the Oceans.* New York, NY: Oxford University Press, 2019.

Abulafia, David. *The Great Sea: A Human History of the Mediterranean.* New York, NY: Oxford University Press, 2013.

Aczel, Amir D. *The Riddle of the Compass: The Invention That Changed the World.* New York, NY: Harcourt, 2001.

Bellis, Mary. "The Compass and Other Magnetic Inventions." ThoughtCo. 2019. https://www.thoughtco.com/compass-and-other-magnetic-innovations-1991466.

Blake, John. *The Sea Chart: The Illustrated History of Nautical Maps and Navigational Charts.* London, UK: Conway Maritime Press, 2016.

Carrick, Phil. "Who Invented the Magnetic Compass?" HistoryDaily.org. 2018. https://historydaily.org/who-invented-the-magnetic-compass.

Editors of Encyclopaedia Britannica. "Compass." Britannica.com. Undated. Retrieved May 2020. https://www.britannica.com/technology/inertial-guidance-system.

Frankopan, Peter. *The Silk Roads: A New History of the World.* New York, NY: Bloomsbury Publishing, 2015.

Gurney, Alan. Compass: *A Story of Exploration and Innovation.* London, UK: Norton, 2004.

National Geographic. "Compass." 2020. https://www.nationalgeographic.org/encyclopedia/compass/.

Needham, Joseph. *The Shorter Science and Civilisation in China, Vol. 3.* Cambridge, UK: Cambridge University Press, 1986.

Paine, Lincoln. *The Sea & Civilization: A Maritime History of the World.* New York, NY: Vintage, 2015.

Richey, Michael William, et al. "Navigation." Britannica.com. Undated. Retrieved May 2020. https://www.britannica.com/technology/navigation-technology/Modern-navigation.

Skinner, Stephen. *Feng Shui History: The Story of Classical Feng Shui in China and the West from 221 BC to 2012 AD.* Woodbury, MN: Llewellyn Publications, 2013.

Stavridis, James. *Sea Power: The History and Geopolitics of the World's* Oceans. New York, NY: Penguin Press, 2017.

Vardalas, John. "A History of the Magnetic Compass." Big History Project. 2019. https://blog.bighistoryproject.com/2019/03/01/a-history-of-the-magnetic-compass/.

Williams, J. E. D. *From Sails to Satellites: The Origin and Development of Navigational Science.* New York, NY: Oxford University Press, 1993.

# Index